# GET ALIGNED!

# GET ALIGNED!

UNLOCKING ENTERPRISE VALUE THROUGH PEOPLE,
PROCESSES AND SYSTEMS

## Alexander Tuff

ISBN: 1974502902
ISBN 13: 9781974502905

# TABLE OF CONTENTS

# FOREWORD

---

I n 2014, I began writing articles for Columbia Business School Magazine on leadership and management and soon realized that after four or five submissions, I was creating the summary guide I wished I'd had before I landed my first senior management role in my early 30s.

During the course of my career I have worked at three multi-billion dollar companies, five start-ups, and two middle-market companies. Through many mistakes and some successes I built out a framework that has worked in every executive role I have held since.

I believe that a collection of basic concepts, like tools in a Swiss Army knife, can enable any leader to make a broad and meaningful impact on an organization. While the chapters that follow are targeted to C-Suite positions, they can be very useful for anyone aspiring to lead in the future. The common thread across topics of people, processes and systems is one of alignment and leadership.

Even if you take just one tool or concept from this book, I'll consider it a success.

Whether you're looking to establishing your mission, vision and values statements, drive efficiency and effectiveness efforts, systemize processes, develop a strategic planning framework, lead offsite retreats or just run effective meetings, this book will help guide you to implement the framework necessary to achieve ultimate alignment.

You'll find yourself making better and faster decisions, shaving off unnecessary work and expenses and continuously improving all aspects of the business. You and your team will collaborate and communicate better than ever before. This will require intense leadership, energy and time, but you will have the basic tools to achieve it.

I hope you enjoy picking up the management tools that I have found so useful in my own career.

*I would like to make a special thanks to my loving wife, Liz, who patiently listens to me about my dreams and ambitions. She gives me the fuel to make ideas come to life and manages to keep me grounded all at the same time. Amazing to be able to spend my life with my best friend and soulmate. And my kids Oliver, Adelaide and Eloise who are the greatest kids a dad could ever ask for.*

*Huge shout out to my sister and very accomplished editor, Sarah Tuff Dunn, for giving her time and advice during the last three years.*

*I offer a huge thank you to all my mentors and peers that helped me formulate these frameworks and inspire me to pull it all the pieces together. The amazing 2003 Cluster X and Columbia Business School editorial staff, Drew Palmer, Tim Tuff, Nat Furman, Juan Navarro-Staicos, Chris Tuff, Campbell Gerrish, Aaron Abrahms, Eric Naison-Phillips, Matt Phillips, Marko Djuranovic, Rohit Dalmia, Tom Neiman, Francie Rawson, Adam Robinson, The Late Professor Biggadike, Doug Smith, Steve Ezzes, Lisa Polsky, Susan Balloch, Dana Ardi, and Rob Rowe. Stamford Hospital Foundation members; Chris Riendeau, Lars Noble, Nick Risom, Andy Merrill, and Ned Burns. Lastly, To the YPO Fairchester Chapter and my dear Forum members: JR Sherman, Steve Obsitnik, Paul Lightbody, Tiffany Kuehner, Cynthia Roy and Jeff Lederer*

*Illustrations provided by Mikaela Becker*

# CHAPTER 1

## 5 Key Concepts for every Operating Executive

Early in my career, I was determined to pick up skills to help me become an effective leader. In 2009, after 15 years accumulating skills, I was appointed to my first true leadership role as chief operating officer (COO) of risk at CIT Group. I oversaw 600 people — and I had only the faintest idea of what to do. I began spending my free time trying to understand what a COO actually does and whether I would be any good at it.

There were plenty of articles about how to succeed as a CEO or a CFO, but there was almost nothing about being a good COO. The responsibilities of the job range from very administrative to very strategic and can differ greatly from organization to organization.

I have now served as an operating executive for three different organizations and have found that there are certain inherent traits that every operating executive possesses, and certain activities and processes that will maximize their impact. Effectiveness is 100 percent correlated with the ability to lead.

Success as a COO also requires some natural inclination for solving complex problems, implementing solutions, and driving change — no matter how big the obstacles might seem. Flexibility while working with diverse teams doesn't hurt. Good communication and collaboration are key. Your effectiveness will also depend on the support of other leaders and your ability to drive change within the organization. Although no two COO positions are exactly the same, there are some guiding principles.

## 1. Identify the key issues.

Every organization has areas for improvement. Meeting with people at every level and asking the right questions will help you identify these issues. By talking with people throughout the organization, you'll improve your decision-making processes. Aggregating and categorizing this information can help you clearly understand organization-wide versus unit-level issues. Surveys can help you get the right information and enable you to measure and articulate key challenges in a noncontroversial way. Using data to illustrate problems or improvements helps remove negative emotions. Prioritize your findings. Identify which tasks require your involvement and delegate the rest. Be transparent and open, solicit feedback, and have an open-door policy. Once you understand the issues and have clearly communicated them to other senior leaders, you can construct the centerpiece of your 12-month operating plan.

## 2. Strive for alignment.

It's no small feat to align behaviors, organizational design, compensation, and goals across a firm. Leaders must agree on the mission, vision, and values of the company. Once there is consensus, you can communicate the company's purpose, direction, and values to your employees. This mission statement will serve as the foundation on which every other alignment effort will be built. With a clear vision, a strong aligned strategic plan can be built, from which a one-year operational plan, departmental goals and individual goals can also be built and highly coordinated. Then it's time to choose an organizational design to support internal communication and collaboration. Clear compensation plans are fundamental. Ensure that there are no morale hazards and that the plans incentivize desired behaviors from each business unit and function. Lastly, alignment ensures the company is moving in the right direction and helps you hold people accountable and reward achievements.

## 3. Find and invest in your best talent.

Operating executives are only as effective as the people they lead. Quickly identify the worst and best performers and cultural supporters. This will require you to follow your gut, even when it means evaluating talent differently than your colleagues. Removing the worst performers and replacing them with the best talent will improve standards across the organization. Give resources to the best talent already in your organization to maximize their impact and ensure their voices are heard. With a solid talent base, you can focus on training them and providing them with opportunities to lead.

## 4. Lead corporate planning efforts.

Helping develop the strategic plan, budget plan, operating plan and project plans gives you the ability to channel resources to the most important efforts. The strategic plan describes what needs to happen over the next three to five years. The budget plan will help you identify where funds can be reprioritized to back the most important projects. The operating plan unifies all departments and should include an IT budget to improve efficiency. Project plans help ensure each unit is working towards firm-wide goals. Make sure you have a seat at the table during the planning process and that your role is clearly understood by all, including yourself.

## 5. Improve everything you touch.

Feedback loops for each process help your organization continuously improve. Identifying waste or unnecessary work will free up resources. Rewarding employees for removing bottlenecks, over-production, and poor prioritization will help create a culture of continuous improvement. Monitor key metrics to understand if goals have been met and improvements are effective. A good operating executive should fill in leadership gaps, fix big issues, and execute core strategy in concert with senior leadership. Most importantly, an operating executive needs to be an effective communicator and collaborator with whom people want to work.

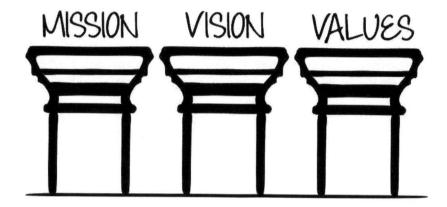

# CHAPTER 2

## MISSION, VISION AND VALUES

At a recent leadership conference I attended, nearly 80 percent of the roughly 400 attendees claimed that their organizations have mission, vision and values statements. But how many of these company representatives actually knew their mission, vision and values statements?

Almost none. Clearly, these statements were neither ingrained into the fabric of their companies nor reinforced every day, rendering them forgettable and ineffective.

Mission, vision, and values statements can guide a firm to great success. The mission statement delineates the company's primary goals; the vision statement explains what the organization hopes to achieve over time; and the values statement lists the qualities and beliefs that the company's employees share.

Together, these statements help employees move in the same direction; ensure their projects and efforts are aligned to a long-term vision; and motivate, attract and retain talent. Faulty and unenforced statements, however, can turn these potentially transformational tools into useless — even harmful — roadblocks that can backfire and weaken a company.

Here are the six essential steps to get it right.

## 1. Get complete buy-in.
The entire leadership team — with input from the rest of the organization, if possible — should help build the mission, vision and values statements in a collaborative and creative exercise. This process alone can help unify the team, bringing to light key differences while drawing out any unhelpful personal agendas. By the end of this process, your company should know both exactly what it wants to be when it grows up and how it plans to get there.

## 2. Set the standard — and live up to it.
Once key values are identified, leaders must ensure that they themselves adhere to them before expecting the same from all employees. Honest apologies can help when employees fail to live up to the organization's values, but individuals who consistently compromise the company's belief system may face termination — even if that person is at the executive level. This shows that the company is serious about its statements and that there is not tolerance for those who do not live by them. It can help to give all employees, including leaders, feedback during the performance process with specific examples of when they did or did not live up to the standards. No one is perfect, but everyone is accountable.

## 3. Don't let statements atrophy.

No matter how fresh they seem when you write them down, words can grow stale. This is especially true when it comes to mission, vision, and values statements. If your statements have turned into outdated, unenforced words on a wall, then you've failed to keep them integrated into the company's culture. Leaders must constantly update and communicate these values through town-hall-style meetings, goals, performance reviews, office reminders, rewards and recognitions.

## 4. Trust decision delegation.

We've all seen leaders who don't trust others to make even the smallest of decisions. But once mission, vision and values statements are successfully in place, everyone should know where the company is headed, and therefore be able to make decisions more easily. Leaders still need to delegate wisely, but streamlined decisions will allow the firm to move much faster — and get a competitive edge.

## 5. Stay on course.

It can be tempting to consider outside ventures, but have faith in the focus that your mission, vision and values statements have brought to the company. Efforts that fall outside of the vision should be dismissed, while opportunities that reinforce the vision should be explored. This clarity will enable the organization to work toward a single point on the horizon.

## 6. Screen new hires for cultural fit.

Your mission, vision and values statements should also clarify what personal qualities you seek in all future employees. This cultural screening process will ensure that new hires are a good fit, which in turn increases pride and morale among employees.

Ultimately, the key to the successful implementation of mission, vision and values statements is strong leadership. Any executive can write these statements, but only a true leader can make these words come alive, live up to them each day, drive them into every aspect of the corporate culture, and deliver the value that they can add to the organization.

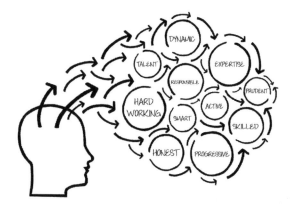

# CHAPTER 3

## GETTING YOUR PEOPLE STRATEGY RIGHT

During my last week at Columbia Business School, my good friend Jesse challenged me to define my career ambitions in one sentence. It didn't take long for me to blurt it out and then write it down so that I would remember: "To unlock the potential of individuals and organizations so that they can realize their fullest possibilities."

But for 10 years, I was so focused on my own ambitions for my organizations that I failed to see the importance of individuals. Like most leaders, I've lost great employees for myriad reasons. They didn't like their manager, for example, or they found another job that paid 15 percent more. I've also hired the wrong people, risking not only the momentum of the organization but also, more importantly (especially for a young organization) its culture.

These experiences have helped me hone in on a critical part of leadership: You can't unlock the potential of an organization without unlocking the potential of its people.

Every firm needs a strategy to recruit, retain, and inspire the best people. Here are seven ways to grow and protect your most valuable asset.

## 1. Get the right people in the right places.

While the wrong leader sits in the window office, the right one may hide behind a cubicle wall. Look for employees' real strengths and move them into the right roles. A top-notch engineer, for example, might be better leaving managerial duties to a trained manager.

Once you have the right leaders in the right places, empower them to rebuild their teams, and trust them to hire people who will complement and enhance existing strengths.

Now is also the time to envision your company's ideal organizational structure, considering its future evolution and growth. Where are the talent gaps? By developing a "future-state" chart, you can clearly see what you need to build during the next six to 12 months.

And sometimes you have to take a deep breath and let a few people go. Which brings us to...

## 2. Let go of the wrong people — and eliminate unnecessary roles.

Identify the people who are no longer contributing to the company in a meaningful way. Challenge the number of layers in the organization and the roles that seem unclear or unnecessary. For example, look for ways multiple teams could fall under one effective leader.

Once you've identified the people to let go, help them find their way out of the organization. Sometimes a candid conversation will help people move on. Alternatively, you may need a round of layoffs to expedite the changes.

## 3. Find new talent with a targeted hiring strategy.

The next step is creating a targeted hiring strategy to bring in new blood. Invest the time and effort in a detailed job description.

Decide whether you want to hire a search firm, use LinkedIn, recruit on college campuses, hire on a "temp-to-permanent" basis, or stage your own episode of "America's Got Talent." The key is to have a plan in place. And remember to spread the word through informal channels, too, with specific desires and, perhaps, specific dollars. Sometimes, a referral fee can help you get the right résumés flowing through the door.

## 4. Screen, screen, screen.

A wide variety of screening tools will fit any company's needs. The point is: Look beyond college prestige and GPA, and use more than one screening tool. Before the interview process even begins, make sure you're interviewing real, authentic potential fits for the position by drilling into candidates' résumés and looking closely at their responsibilities and achievements at prior organizations. Do they have the experience necessary to succeed, or will someone have to hold their hand for a year?

I recommend personality tests such as Kolbe, along with intelligence tests such as Wonderlic, to reveal the candidates' hidden strengths and weaknesses. If the position requires math skills, give a math test. If it requires writing skills, give a writing test. Doing the tests onsite offers insight about a candidate's ability to handle time pressure.

Most importantly, screen for the culture of your company. Will they be able to live up to the standards and values of the organization? Will they fit in with others? In the face-to-face interviews, ask them how they would respond to different situations to see if they truly believe in your organization's values and standards. Also make sure that all interviewers are using the same set of standards and rating criteria so that the best possible debriefing conversations happen.

While no single screen will provide all the information you need to know about a candidate, collectively they can be helpful signals that indicate whether the individual will be an asset or a liability.

## 5. Have a development plan for every employee.

Education and training that are prerequisites for many positions can take several years and many thousands of dollars. So why should it end when your employee walks in the front door the first day on the job? Your company must create a professional development plan (with specific guidelines for goals and the skills to get employees there) as the employees integrate themselves into their new roles.

Good development plans include relevant training as well as participation in firm-wide projects, such as a lunch & learn, that can help employees absorb the company's culture and knowledge. Professional development should also be part of the annual review process; every year, employees and managers should revisit these blueprints to make the necessary adjustments for success.

Performing skill-gap analysis across the firm can also help managers develop a training program customized to the firm's needs. What specific skills and knowledge do various functions or groups need to be successful, and how does the existing team align with those measurements? Training may include Excel shortcuts, financial modeling, or a workshop on how to write an effective email.

Remember that training is an investment in your most important asset; don't under-budget this line item.

## 6. Hold on tight to your talent.

When a key employee leaves, it can drain value from your company more than you know. So how can you prevent the best people from departing?

First, ensure strong communication between high-potential employees and managers. Are employees' expectations being met? Try using informal lunches, happy hour outside the office, or an occasional walk through a nearby park as a way to stay connected to your employees to make sure members of the company are keeping up with their professional ambitions. Sure, their talent may sometimes grow beyond the demands of the job, but that's where flexibility is essential. Perhaps a six-month project will give them the exposure and experience necessary for that next internal job. Help them identify a clear career path within the organization to ensure that they are actively engaged and growing.

As long as employees are growing, they're more likely to stay; money is not the key retention factor. Envision success as your ability to unlock the talent of others and you will create and inspire future leaders in any organization. Recognize and celebrate high-achieving employees to reinforce positive behavior and keep morale high.

## 7. Be ready to pounce.

This comes down to having a flexible budget so you can seize the opportunity when that perfect candidate becomes available.

Communicate that you are always looking for the best and brightest talent out there even if there are no formal positions available.

This can help bring in leaders for new key projects, or even new lines of business that you would otherwise not be able to pursue.

**A few final words...**

Integrate your people strategy into your strategic plan. This will provide clarity not only to the executive level, but also to everyone in the company. People can go from your biggest pain to your greatest relief when you simply take the time to focus on your approach. And if you become a place that becomes known as a breeding ground for top talent, you'll get even better talent coming through the door.

# CHAPTER 4

## 10 Ways to Create a Culture of Open Communication

I t was a silly argument with my wife about leaving dirty dishes in the sink that my 9-year-old son, Oliver, overheard. I was satisfied with my side, but when I put Oliver to bed that night, he rehashed the heated exchange, point by point, explaining how I didn't see things from my wife's perspective.

He explained how he'd seen her frustration growing for months; no matter how many times she told me to clean up, I never did. Taking a step back, I could see that the feedback my son was giving me was absolutely right and that I needed to change my ways and improve the way I listen and communicate with my wife on matters that are of concern to her. (It's a work in progress.)

While our kitchen conversation was of little consequence to global matters, companies around the world can face major setbacks when they don't have standard processes and channels in place for employees to give and receive feedback.

Creating a culture of open communication is one of the best ways to inspire excellent performance, improve employee morale, and foster a warmer corporate culture. Here are 10 simple ways to integrate feedback into your company.

## 1. Around-the-Clock Clear Communication Channels

Ask your direct reports how you are doing as a manager and what they like — and don't like. In the meantime, stay vigilant about continuously reinforcing their strengths and flagging weaknesses. Prompt feedback means that issues are resolved immediately.

Avoid email: messages can be misunderstood, misguided, or missed altogether. Communicate in person or, if necessary, over the phone.

## 2. Weekly One-on-One Meetings

Keep a standing date with each direct report. These informal chats will allow concerns to be addressed without interrupting the rest of your week. Don't stand your date up: you'll be seen as inaccessible or direct reports will feel like less of a priority, which can muddy the feedback process.

## 3. Monthly or Quarterly Staff Meetings

This is a chance to share key information like board decisions and new initiatives with all employees. Time these meetings when you have information to share, such as several days after a board meeting. Be sure to make the gatherings enjoyable. For example, you might begin with a relevant story or by recognizing an employee's recent accomplishment. Boredom or bossiness will alienate your audience. Allow time for a Q&A

session. By the end of each meeting, your team should be in-the-know and have their key concerns or questions addressed.

## 4. Annual Reviews

These should be formal one-on-one sit-downs, with consistent standards measuring each employee's performance. If your organization has had poor feedback strategies in the past, be prepared for some resistance on annual reviews — and reassure staff members that the goal is positive outcomes, not negative reprimands. I have experienced this firsthand when a teary-eyed employee asked to discontinue annual reviews because they made everyone nervous, angry, or sad. Turning that around by opening up more ongoing channels for employee feedback means that everyone will know where they stand before annual reviews take place, making the process a less anxious experience for everyone.

## 5. Anonymous Surveys

Surveys make it possible to regularly assess your firm's culture and employees' overall happiness. I also use them to measure employee engagement, and I share results and trends with the entire organization. Anonymity is important — employees need to feel comfortable speaking their minds — as is closing the loop: you should be prepared to respond to employees' feedback. Our company Intranet allows surveys and voting to be completely transparent, which helps create a culture of trust while driving home the message that everyone is invited to identify opportunities for improvement.

## 6. 360-Degree Reviews

One spring, I underwent a 360-degree review and realized that my own progress as a leader was hampered because I was not addressing the most critical opportunities for growth. It was a bit painful — as 360-degree reviews can be — but showed me how to correct my course. A licensed professional should conduct 360-degree reviews, discuss feedback, and offer positive advice for improvement.

## 7. Post-Mortem Debriefs

These are meetings focused on internal assessment of major projects or deals — both what was successful and what can be done better the next time around. These check-ins allow the firm to capture key learnings for the next big deal or project and to turn challenging issues into opportunities for improvement. Remember to accentuate the good along with the bad.

## 8. Informal Social Outings

Whether it's a trip to the local bowling alley or a picnic lunch in Central Park, get-togethers outside the office are a chance to loosen up. To avoid getting *too* informal, keep after-work drinks to one and done.

## 9. State-of-the-Union E-mail Communications

While trying to keep email to essentials, every so often —say, once a quarter —I e-mail all staff members on the strategic direction of the organization or company values. These messages are an important way to keep everyone at the firm in touch with the bigger picture beyond individual functions or teams.

## 10. Employee Exit Interviews

Regardless of your organization's size, make sure that departing employees are interviewed about their experiences and reasons for leaving. People are often very open in these interviews, which provide incredibly valuable feedback. Take employees' comments seriously and ask your HR team to present trends and takeaways from exit interviews to management annually so that actions can be taken to help retain valuable employees and increase overall morale.

Creating a culture of open communication takes work, like any relationship, and is easily overlooked when business is humming along. Any one of these tools is a start and is well worth the effort to drive a company to new levels of productivity and employee happiness.

# CHAPTER 5

## 4 STEPS TO MAKE MEETINGS WORK

We've all suffered the malaise — death by a million meaningless internal meetings. Internal meetings can be directionless and leaderless time-wasters that kill productivity and cause dread and fear among employees. Or, they can be highly functioning productive meetings — if you plan carefully.

These four steps will turn your meetings into must-haves.

### 1. Prepare for the Meeting

Select one leader to call for the meeting, prepare an agenda — with any special notes or presentations attached — and oversee the proceedings. Everyone else attending, meanwhile, should review these materials. A meeting coordinator can help with logistics.

## 2. Start the Meeting

On time! Like it or not, the clock tick-tocks success. If your train is five minutes late, it sets you back. Same with meetings. Encourage punctuality by placing a "fine bucket" in the meeting room and requiring latecomers to deposit $5. Record their rudeness next to the name on the notes distributed to everyone after the meeting — I guarantee they will get it. Before you get into the nitty-gritty, state the purpose, goals, and allocated time. Why are you all in a room together?

## 3. Manage the Meeting

Clarity should prevail, from point A to point B. If someone presents something ambiguous, speak up! "When you said, 'Conquer the world,' did you really mean, 'Sell 100,000 units by year-end?' Strict time checks every 10 to 15 minutes will keep the meeting aligned and on schedule. Watch closely for digressions and move the fluffy stuff off the table in favor of relevant topics. A "parking lot" can hold important, but irrelevant points, while a note on follow-up meetings optimize everyone's time. Appoint a scribe to capture all key points made.

## 4. Close the Meeting

Do. Not. Look. At. The. Door. Instead, use the last burst of energy to review the Next Steps. What needs to be done? Who is responsible? And when will it be completed by? Allow yourself a buffer zone of 5 to 10 minutes, ending the meeting early so that loose threads can be tied up and everyone can get back to their desks. Within 24 hours, send meeting notes, copying all necessary parties.

The Prep, Start, Manage, and Close format will make your meetings more productive and could begin to bend the company's culture away from death by a million meaningless internal meetings. Good luck!

## Four Stages of Running an Effective Meeting

### PREPARE FOR THE MEETING

- AGENDA: Always have an agenda with topics and allocated times
- Bring in PRIOR MEETING NOTES
- ASSIGN ROLES: Meeting coordinator and meeting scribe
- MATERIAL: Meeting materials should be sent before the meeting

### START THE MEETING

- Start the meeting ON TIME
- At the start of each meeting, define:
  - PURPOSE and goals of the meeting
  - Total TIME SCHEDULED for the meeting

### MANAGE THE MEETING

- CLARIFY, CLARIFY, CLARIFY: Meeting coordinator is expected to get full clarity from the group
- TIME CHECK: Meeting coordinator to perform "time checks" every 10-15 minutes
- TABLE OFF-TOPIC DISCUSSION: Manage digressions and table off-topic conversations for later

### CLOSE THE MEETING

- Clarify NEXT STEPS and "to-dos"
- Get meeting FEEDBACK
- END EARLY: Shoot to end the meeting ten minutes early
- SEND MEETING MINUTES to all participants and absentees

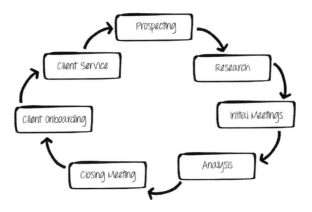

# CHAPTER 6

## PROCESS SYSTEMIZATION

I'm sure I'm not the only one who feels like I'm living "Groundhog Day." It seems that every morning, I arrive at work to find that same person asking for time off or a paycheck even though I've explained the process many times before.

These repetitive questions run you down and can make you believe that you are the only one that can do the job, forcing you to micromanage the organization. You can also stop wishing that there were four more people out there that you could hire and trust to perform these efforts you have no energy for — because they aren't out there, and there's an easier way to do things.

By documenting your processes and aligning them to the organization's vision, you'll give yourself the ability to move out of the details and into the higher value-creating roles in the organization, and even let the processes strengthen the company as it grows. Additionally, by documenting the company's "secret sauce," you will enable your firm to maintain consistent high quality work.

## What in my firm is actually a process?

If you take a bird's eye view of what goes on in an organization, you begin to realize that a majority of all efforts in your organization are simply part of connected cycles, a system that has a beginning and an end. Some are not as apparent as others, but once you recognize the full set of "cycles," you can build out the processes and procedures, and, with some TLC, you'll be able to get yourself out of "Groundhog Day," clear up any confusion across all employees, get the senior team focused on higher valued work, reduce variances of quality, and help move an organization out of the Dark Ages and into the world where everything you do is systematized, documented automated wherever possible.

Documented processes and procedures also cut down employee training time, allowing for quicker integration of new employees, and a reduction in the disruption to the employee's manager and team during onboarding. They also break down silos of information, lessening the impact of losing any individual employee.

For example, the sales pipeline is a process. Each stage of the pipeline can be defined and the requirements and steps to complete the process can made clear. Various stages can be broken down even further to make sure that each step is both manageable and actionable.

Here are quick and easy steps to get your growing organization systematized.

## 1. Set a goal and timeframe and get the required buy-in

As for any project that you launch, you must first identify the goals for mapping out the processes and procedures of the firm. This will require internal and potentially external resources, so it needs to justify the time you spend.

That said, some simple goals for this project could include:

- Ensuring that each process has an owner
- Reducing variation of quality of the work product
- Allowing senior management to capture data
- Decreasing the speed and increasing the effectiveness of training new employees on their role and expectations
- Identifying and addressing bottlenecks in the organization
- Systematizing everything possible
- Looking for opportunities for automation

Mapping out processes can be very time-consuming and could take months for a group or team to complete, given the other demands on their time. But it can result in an operational manual that lays out all processes across the organization and serves as a reference guide for all employees.

Before you embark on such a process, try training a cross-functional team on process mapping or six-sigma so that there is a squad addressing the problem all speaking the same language rather than any single individual who will likely be overwhelmed and under-supported.

Senior members of the organization should communicate the importance of the project.

## 2. Schedule a brainstorming session.
Getting the employees who actually do the work into a room can allow for effective mapping of processes. Often these conversations highlight the full process for the department for the very first time. A recent

brainstorming session in my company raised dozens of unnecessary steps and very simple things such as having frequently-called phone numbers automated on the phone system. It also adjusted the final report output to a PDF rather than a hard copy. Additionally, it allowed a department to dive further into each step of the process to identify potential methods to control the quality and output.

We also used a well-known approach of having teams lay out Post-it notes so any individual could move the steps around, simplify tasks or suggest where manual processes could be automated.

## 3. Document "current state" processes.

Once you've completed all brainstorming sessions, it's time to document all the processes using the same methodology. Each process will have a starting point and an ending point. This will allow any single person in the organization to understand the processes across all areas. It may be tempting to jump ahead to put a more efficient process in place, but to start, it's critical to get the current process nailed as there will be many areas for improvements.

Look to connect processes across the organization. Often one process leads to another, and those processes should note the connection.

Look to capture a process step that has a series of requirements with a procedure that may be a step–by–step guide or checklist. Whether it's opening up the office for a new day, onboarding a new employee or replenishing supplies in the kitchen, simple tasks within a larger process often have a series of steps that can be controlled with a simple checklist to ensure everything is completed. Checklists remove the inconsistency that comes from people forgetting a step. They can also be incredibly powerful guides for anyone in the organization from an EA to the CEO.

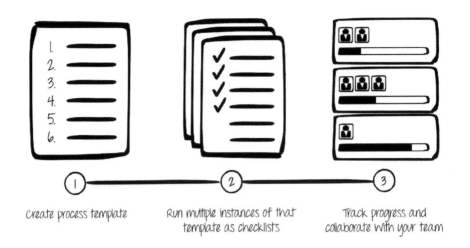

| Create process template | Run multiple instances of that template as checklists | Track progress and collaborate with your team |

Take time to get it right. Build the first department as your "guinea pig" example, and then replicate through the other units. As you document out the process, note where there are owners to a process and where there are not.

The most important part is to get it all down on paper.

## 4. Set a desired "future state" for processes.

Like any other project that you manage, there will be a current state and future state of processes within departments and an organization. With the right leadership, your firm can undergo process re-engineering to accomplish the desired future state. Easy questions to ask as the process owners develop the future state are:

- Where can processes be simplified?
- Where are the bottlenecks hitting in the organization?
- Are there people who have too much work assigned?
- Are there processes that could be working in parallel with one another rather than sequentially?
- Where can coordination of calendars help avoid jamming up organizational processes?

- Would implementation of a task tracking system make it easier to manage ad hoc and repetitive tasks?
- Where can processes be automated?
- Are there opportunities to add workflow solutions instead of paper going from one desk to the next?
- Do the processes have a beginning and an end, and are they digestible by a new employee?
- Where can we add templates, policies, procedures, process maps, and checklists?
- Are there opportunities to add controls such as a review or approval?

## 5. Capture processes in a consolidated location.

Creating a centralized repository of processes allows any organization to easily update processes and allow for the supporting documents for the Corporate Operating Manual. Each process should be reviewed on some regular interval to ensure that they are kept up to date. This manual is the company's secret sauce, the intellectual property that drives real enterprise value. Remove key-man risk around those folks who are the "only ones who know how to do something" and get the repeatable processes such as payroll, expenses, onboarding, time tracking locked down once and for all. Ideally this would be on a company's intranet where it is easily accessible. You don't want it buried in a hard copy binder that gets dusty and ultimately thrown away.

## 6. Focus on continuous improvement.

Once all the processes are documented and the firm moves toward a future state, there will be additional process improvement ideas that come up along the way. Capture all the ideas and encourage employees to submit ideas as they think of them. Once documented the process owner can begin to surgically adjust processes instead of making a change on the fly. There can also be data collected on the processes that give key performance indicators and other data to highlight opportunities for improvement, whether that is adding additional resources, or just ad-justing a process.

It will also allow the processes owners to drill into the processes in a more granular level as problems arise. These deep dives give transpar-ency into areas of concern and adjustments required to stop the leaky pipe and keep the system running smoothly. Additionally, as issues arise the owners can quickly identify whether or not the issue is a people issue or a process issue.

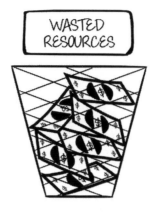

# CHAPTER 7

## IDENTIFYING WASTED RESOURCES

W e're all guilty of it. My kids toss a half-eaten grilled cheese in the rubbish. My wife leaves all the lights on when we leave the house to go skiing. And me? I buy an espresso machine that I'll never use.

It's all waste.

But once you start looking in the right places — which is, granted, a bit more complicated than looking in the trash bin or at the electricity bill — finding and eradicating waste in the workplace can transform both the top-line and bottom-line results.

So that you don't waste your own time, here are nine areas on which to shine the spotlight and nix workplace waste.

## 1. Delays

No matter how efficient you believe your company to be, chances are there are bottlenecks slowing down the process of getting goods and services to the client. So start tracking turnaround times and comparing those to the expectations. ID the delays and destroy them.

## 2. Errors

Maybe you make fleece jackets. Maybe you provide financial advice. Either way, when you don't pay attention to the tiny details, you create mistakes. And mistakes cost money — along with those dreaded delays and the potential for a ruined reputation. If errors or defects are becoming a pattern, drill into the root cause. It may require a new machine or perhaps may be as simple as investing the time in training employees on how to optimally perform a certain task.

## 3. Underutilized staff

Remember when you welcomed that talented new hire? Chances are, at some point he or she is feeling underutilized or even underemployed. So talk to employees, face to face, and keep a suggestion box near the water cooler. Get the right people in the right work.

## 4. Inventories

Unless you are a real cereal killer, you don't have 20 boxes of Frosted Flakes in your cabinets, and 20 gallons of 2 percent in your fridge. Does the same common sense reign in your office? Determine optimal inventories for each cycle, from your product to paper and print cartridges to cash and even permanent employees. You may have an oversupply of labor that could be solved by temps.

## 5. Processes

It's that head-smacking moment from the v8 commercial. You should have asked two people, not three, to proofread someone's work. You make 10 different sizes of a T-shirt when you only need four. You should have used an e-signature instead of FedExing those papers. You have five people interview a candidate before rather giving them the writing or math test that they fail. These are all poor processes. Once a year, examine each and every process to make sure it works efficiently for business. Simplify or stop those that don't. Consider placing an expiration date on a process to ensure a certain frequency of review.

## 6. Overproducing

A 100-page customized presentation is useless for a client that only requested two pages. Overdoing anything wastes resources and compromises your credibility. Spend less time crafting clever emails or coming up with examples for a client. KISS: Keep it simple, stupid.

# CHAPTER 8

## 13 Ways to Better Manage Expenses

From splurging on a new pair of Nikes to flashing a credit card for a Caribbean vacation, let's face it: spending can be fun. But overspending in your business is, well, just plain dumb. Managing expenses effectively is one of the most important steps for long-term success — and it's where so many of us stumble.

Here are 13 ideas to help you right-size your expenses.

### 1. Harness your headcount.
People cost money. To start, **outsource where you can**. As an example, my company recently outsourced technology support and development, which saved us 60 percent in costs and significantly accelerated our ability to implement new software.

Meanwhile, get rid of the **underperformers,** the **overvalued,** and the **sacred cows** who are taking away more value than they're worth. You may also be overpaying people, so consider a **compensation study** to determine fair salaries.

Larger companies will want to dive into their **spans and layers.** For example, if the CEO manages 5 directs and each of them manages 5 directs, then you need only 5 **layers** for a company of 700 people. In a firm of this size, identify all the people who manage fewer than 5 people **(span of control)** and parts of the organization that have more than 5 layers of management. Then look for specific opportunities to remove layers, combine responsibilities into fewer roles, and reduce people.

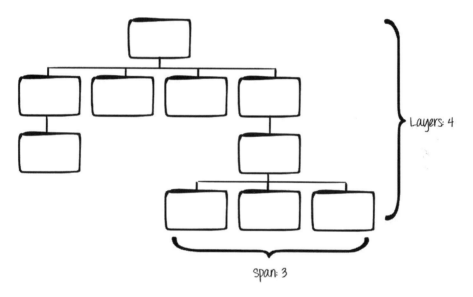

Layers: 4

span: 3

A final way to harness your headcount is to **set targeted front-office-to-back-office ratios.** This can allow managers to see when you may be back-office heavy. Whether it's 1:1 or 1:5, having a ratio upon which senior management agrees will force everyone to look for opportunities to rein in expenses even further.

## 2. Use interns.

If you get the right ones this can be the best bang for your compensation buck, as they can take on simple but time-consuming tasks. Young and hungry interns can take on those lower-value tasks and allow other employees to focus on higher-value work that is commensurate with their experience and compensation.

## 3. Move middle or back office workers to lower-cost locations.

I've seen companies save $50 million or more by moving Manhattan-paying jobs to Jacksonville and Salt Lake City. It's a longer-term strategy, but it works.

## 4. Promote telecommunicating.

Some of our best employees have worked out of home offices in India, Switzerland and the West Coast. Thanks in large part to teleconferencing and instant messaging, sometimes I never know that they're not in the main office. By having people work outside the office, you can look to rent smaller space or sublet the space you no longer need. In addition, you may be able to negotiate lower compensation for people who work out of lower cost locations.

## 5. Negotiate and find buying power with vendors.

Everything is still negotiable. Expensive black-car services? We were recently able to cut that cost by talking our car service into matching Über's prices. For small businesses, consortium groups can help pull together purchasing power to negotiate lower rates for everything from office supplies to healthcare costs. A professional employer organization, or PEO, that takes on your HR functions can also reduce healthcare costs. Finally, use corporate credit cards rather than checks to pay vendors. This will save time and accrue air miles, which can then be used to pay some expenses.

Negotiating with vendors is also a good way to reduce professional fees. Freelance lawyers might be looking for part-time work and might charge a fraction of what you're paying people on retainer. If you want to keep a firm on retainer, find out what other firms charge and use that information to renegotiate your rates.

## 6. Focus on the overtime.

How much are you paying? Shifting work hours can minimize this expense line. If you're in an industry where the overtime hours are racking up, consider shifting hours around, bringing in a temp or even another intern to keep the line item in check.

## 7. Reengineer the process.

A tighter and leaner organization comes from improving automation and simplifying processes to free up resources. Lose unnecessary reports and useless weekly emails, and make a long-term investment in a well-run system with no extra clutter.

## 8. Stay focused on business, not hobbies.

You might be overpaying for potential product lines and projects that are just pipe dreams. Remain more fully committed to profitable ventures instead. Allow your company to finish less crucial projects only if you make it to certain revenue or profitability targets halfway through the year.

## 9. Let the experts develop the software.

Expensive IT projects can be a costly trap; cut the cord on those you already know are failures or need some serious maintenance every year. Instead of spending $20K a year upgrading your customized software program and paying dearly for an offsite disaster recovery location, consider using an out-of-the-box software solution that has annual upgrades from which you can benefit.

## 10. Split the cost of events.

Other vendors or partners might be willing to share branding and speaking opportunities at costly conferences. Or, for internal events, consider combining events into one, such as a joint 50th anniversary and a holiday party.

## 11. Lose the paper addiction.

Ink, paper, waste: What can you move to the digital realm that will share the same exact information in a better format? Show your work on a screen and maintain commonly asked-for material on your iPad or computer so that you can send information with ease, instead of constantly printing out the material for every meeting.

## 12. Become creative with space.

Perhaps you can sublet your space to help offset the office costs. If you're downsizing, leave a lease early, and find cheaper and smaller space. If you are getting a new space, consider doing an office share so you can split the overhead costs. Analyze your space use and other large expense items separately and on a regular basis to more clearly identify opportunities to save.

## 13. Cut the travel and entertainment budget.

You can still schedule trips, but pack them with more meetings, and implement limits on hotel costs. When possible, organize teleconferences or webinars. Avoid sending the entire sales team to one conference. Consider selling those pricey, unused season tickets and instead, when you need to, use Stub Hub to get those front-row tickets. Maintain a strict standard on expenses; for example, require senior management approval for any expense more than $500.

Reeling in expenses can be one of the hardest parts of running a business. There are probably cost savings you haven't even thought of yet. Consider offering $1,000 to employees for the best idea that achieves an expense cut, or reward such an idea in a non-monetary way, such as giving the winning employee the chance to join an important project. Tie individual and department goals and incentive rewards to the expense line, and let everyone — from department heads to employees — know that everyone has a stake in managing the bottom line.

# CHAPTER 9

MEET THE BUSINESS INTELLIGENCE AND REPORTING
NEEDS OF YOUR GROWING ORGANIZATION

B efore I even started at my current firm, I requested copies of all of the reports the firm produced. The reports gave me information into the firm's past and future, and helped me identify gaps where key information was missing.

Reports and readily available data are like lights on a pilot's dashboard indicating where the opportunities and issues are, the current state, and where you could end up if issues are not addressed. Without data and reporting, all decisions are just a gut feeling.

In many growing organizations, the pilot's dashboard is not fully built out. By following a simple six-step approach, you can transform your reporting, which will enable you to fix and adjust your company on the fly.

## Step 1: Align to the vision.

The primary purpose of reporting is to help the company achieve its desired vision. As the saying goes, "If you don't know where you are going, any road will get you there." Once there is a clear vision for the firm, all reporting can be designed to align to that vision. For example, if your vision is to become five times the size in revenues with no product errors over three years, then the reporting can focus on all of the elements that will help you achieve that vision.

## Step 2: Define the reporting.

Getting agreement at the board and senior management level around the purpose and goals of reporting will help the firm focus on achieving those goals. In a recent organization that I helped lead, we agreed on the key elements for all reporting across the organization. We defined reporting as putting the right information in front of the right people at the right time. Therefore, "reporting" covered everything from a hard copy board report to real-time information on sales and production available through a mobile device.

The constituents that we focused on included everyone from departmental heads, senior management, the board of directors, shareholders, employees, clients and regulators.

## Step 3: Define the reporting requirements.

In a recent role, we defined the goals of reporting as follows:

1. Transparency. Successful reporting will provide the necessary transparency for key decisions to be made.
2. Strong Data Quality. All data needs to be fresh, accurate and material. As they say, garbage in, garbage out.
3. User-Friendly. Once collected, the data needs to be synthesized, summarized and easy to digest for the audience.

4. Relevant and Audience-Specific. Typically, the higher up you go, the more distilled the information needs to be. Boards often **receive integrated reporting** that allows them to see all facets of the business in a summarized format. This enables them to ask the important questions and dig deeper into the areas of most concern, and make recommendations or decisions based on the data and reports presented.

5. Timeliness. Often you want data that is real-time and predictive of what lies ahead, not just what has already happened. So toss the stale stuff, and focus instead on fresh data to drive decisions.

6. Actionable. The right data at the right time will give the appropriate parties the information they need to make informed decisions.

7. Coordinated. The timing of reports should be coordinated so that the reports and information flow up to the board level, and then the process begins again. Report frequency may vary from daily to annually below the board, but the key information is captured and shared up through the organization.

## Step 4: Determine the types of reports to consider.

The following are examples of typical core reports that are used to provide both financial and operational transparency.

- **Financial Budgeting and Projections.** A strong **budget** report will provide:
  - Actual vs. projections
  - Breakdowns of larger expense categories
  - Liquidity analysis
  - Forward-looking projections
- In a larger financial reporting package you may see **expense breakouts** of larger line items, **Profitability analysis** of different product lines and clients, **Hiring forecasts**, and breakouts of **line items that are over budget**.
- Within the finance department there will likely be more reporting activity on other treasury areas such as wires and any

movement of money. Reviewing these reports can also act as a control around potential fraudulent activity.

- **Integrated Reporting** includes reports on operational elements of the business beyond the financials such as compliance, regulatory, human resources, strategy, governance and environmental.
- **Flash Reports** can be daily or weekly. They provide senior managers insight to the sales activity of the day, production, inventory, and revenue collection. The better the repository system, the easier it is to extract the data.
- **Pipeline Reports** give both the sales team and the executive team visibility into projected revenues. These can also be used to gut check the projections to see if they are realistic. Allocating percentage likelihood of close can give greater comfort around the numbers being provided.
- **Client Reporting** can include monthly reporting on investment returns and aggregated summary purchase reports.
- **Strategic Plan and Project Reporting**. Project statuses can be very simply reported with a "Green, Amber, Red" status. A green status doesn't need much attention, but amber and red need further explanation. This is an easy way to get updates on the most important projects in the organization.
- **Key Performance Indicators and Dashboard reporting.** These are some of the best lights on the pilot's dashboard. By capturing the 3 to 5 key metrics in each area of the business, a manager or executive can see where the areas of concern are, ask the right questions, and dig deeper if appropriate. This streamlines a lot of activity into a critical few pieces to consider. For example, in the production line it might be: number of produced boxes, number of defects, percentage utilization and percentage downtime.

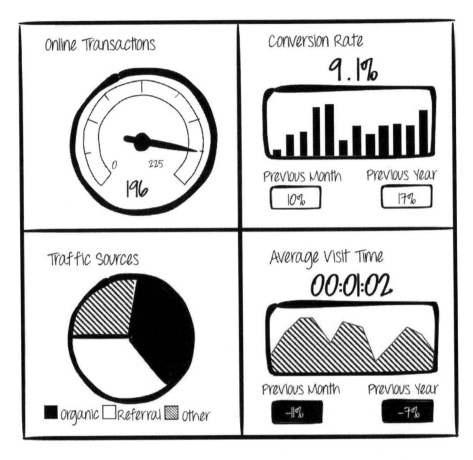

- **Ad Hoc reporting** includes the requested reports and deeper dives into troubled areas — for example, looking into exposure in a certain region such as Canada or Australia.
- In all board reports there should be a placeholder for any major material occurrences or concerns at the management level. If other reports do not pick something up, then it needs to be added.
- Outside third parties may also be hired to provide annual reports such as an **Audit Report**, a **Compliance Review** or **Controls Audit**.
- **Regulatory Reporting.** Depending on the business, there may be a requirement around regulatory reporting

## Step 5: Develop the future state of the organizations reporting infrastructure.

I was a COO at one company that had 29 different receivable systems that collectively stored the information of millions of transactions. But none of the receivable systems were connected, the data collected was different across the board, and very few people in the organization knew how to even get at the data. This left the senior management, shareholders and board completely in the dark.

But by building a desired future state we were soon able to develop a data warehouse that pulled all newly verified data into one place, and through out of the box software it synthesized a summary dashboard for senior management that had drill-down capabilities. The transformation was tremendous. Not to mention, old reports that took hundreds of hours to complete with questionable data were eliminated. Data integrity must be a focus.

The more digital, the better; getting website analytics is as simple as a click of a mouse with Google Analytics. Ideally all information would be this easy and updated. Interactive data has drill-down capabilities using software tools such as Qlikview. For example, you can see revenue exposure by state, then county, town, and even individual purchase. It all depends of the data that you are trying to capture. But the easier the data is to manipulate, the fewer ad-hoc hard copy reports you'll need to make, cutting back the significant amount of resources required to complete such a request. If there isn't an off-the-shelf reporting solution, consider investing in a customized solution. Having the right systems that can pull data quickly can make the difference of having a team of 5 people versus 1.

## Step 6: Determine best way to deliver the reports.

When someone says "reporting," we often imagine a bunch of people dressed up around a table looking at paper or charts on a screen. Today, however, we can share reporting information with the respective constituents in many ways: email as an attachment or in the body of the email, secured portal, intranet, video conference, interactive reporting via iPads and, of course, meetings.

With improved reporting, the leadership team can begin to fix the plane in flight. But be forewarned, there will be turbulence!

## Tips and Tricks

- Review the full suite of reports on an annual basis and make sure they are all still worth the cost to create them; brainstorm new reports that help decision-making and value creation.
- Use call-outs around key numbers and changes, and use narratives.
- Make sure the report tells a story and doesn't just produce lots of numbers and information.
- Figure out the story and summarize it.
- Make your reports simple and digestible.
- Be sure to password-protect confidential reports that you send via email.
- Create a committee that is responsible for reporting and data integrity.
- Establish a balance between frequency and detail.
- Make the reports searchable on an intranet or portal.
- Explore business intelligence software programs that could revolutionize the way your firms accesses and uses data.
- For regulators or other outside parties, try to leverage the internal reports as much as possible.
- Make reports accessible through all devices.

# CHAPTER 10

## 5 Steps to Managing Risk in your Growing Company

We all make mistakes. When I was working for a hedge fund, I watched one trader sell a bond to another trader — three doors away in the same office. Yep, the middleman trader who earned a 2 percent fee from both sides of the trade must still be laughing today.

I once witnessed an extra zero mistakenly added to a 5,000-share transaction cost a firm tens of thousands of dollars. And yet another unnamed company was still making $10 million loans at the same exact time it was facing a liquidity crisis and ended up in bankruptcy.

The only surefire way to avoid silly mistakes is through building a robust governance and controls environment. These words no longer belong only to large regulated organizations. Any growing company that wants to survive the ever-increasing world of risks — from fraud to cyberterrorism — can manage and mitigate these by taking simple steps to protect the business.

This 5-step process guides the development of a governance and controls framework using basic project management tools — protecting you from the very risks that your organization faces.

## Step 1: List and map your risks.

What is the full spectrum of risks that your young and growing firm faces? Many are not obvious at first. Start by listing all the situations where things have gone wrong in the past and all the worries that keep you up at night, from that vice president who cheated on his expense report to the virus that shut down your computers for two days. A good way to get a jump-start on key risks is to obtain a vendor or bank due-diligence list and review their most pressing concerns.

Separate risks into internal (inside the organization) and external (facing the company from the outside). Examples of internal risks include: retaining top staff and key persons, social media, client concentration, lack of succession planning, diminishing brands, legal suits, compliance failures, IT security breach data entry/trade errors, intellectual property loss and data integrity.

Examples of external risks include: regulatory changes, reputational risk, headline risk, competitive market disruption, legislative risks, fraud risk (such as an external party stealing money), margin compression, facility shutdown from weather and data security breach.

A great way to capture the internal and external risks is with a basic risk map that calibrates likelihood of a risk occurring and the loss should an event occur. Once you've laid out the key risks, you can figure out the various tools that will help you put controls around those risks.

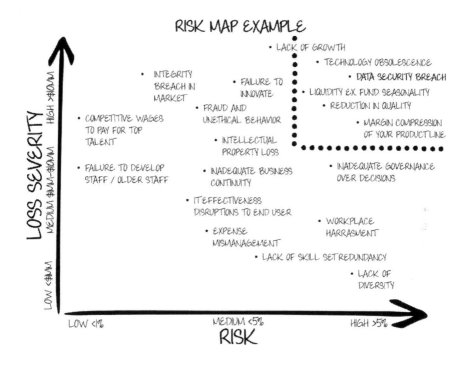

RISK MAP EXAMPLE

## Step 2: Develop your governance and controls framework.

An effective governance and controls framework is a set of mitigation efforts to address everyday risks in a very thoughtful and targeted way. This diagram shows a suite of tools that can be used across your company's culture, people, processes and tools.

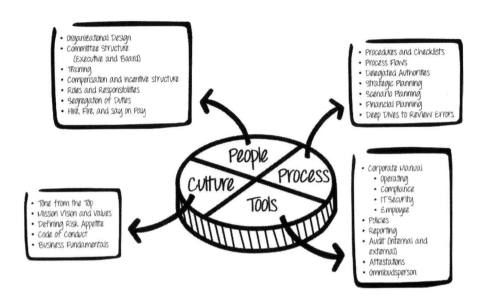

- Organizational Design
- Committee Structure (Executive and Board)
- Training
- Compensation and incentive structure
- Roles and Responsibilities
- Segregation of Duties
- Hire, Fire, and Say on Pay

- Procedures and Checklists
- Process Flows
- Delegated Authorities
- Strategic Planning
- Scenario Planning
- Financial Planning
- Deep Dives to Review Errors

- Tone from the Top
- Mission Vision and Values
- Defining Risk Appetite
- Code of Conduct
- Business Fundamentals

- Corporate Manual
  - Operating
  - Compliance
  - IT Security
  - Employee
- Policies
- Reporting
- Audit (internal and external)
- Attestations
- Ombudsperson

## Step 3: Describe your current state and your desired future state.

How are processes being completed today, and how can they strengthen and improve in the future? This high-level plan allows the senior team to see where you're headed and why it is so important.

With your controls in place, you'll become more efficient and effective in shifting from your current state to your desired future state. In one of my former companies, for example, an employee was spending 100 percent of her time reconciling all credit cards and wire transfers across the organization. We examined the process and determined a different approach that could be completed electronically — and in 10 percent of the time.

Automated processes reduce manual errors. Procedures will reduce variation of output, data will become much more reliable, and transparency into data and reporting will allow for better and quicker decision-making. As you grow your enterprise, stay tuned to how you adapt your governance and controls to mitigate new emerging and changing risks.

## Step 4: Develop a customized action plan to serve as your project management tool.

This is your project management tool, one that will allow you to implement and build out of the desired future state framework and infrastructure. Dozens of software tools, such as Microsoft Project, Google Project Management, Slack, Wrike, Trello and Asana, can maintain tabs on all your projects and assigned tasks.

With a plan in place, you'll be able to track various projects, assign out responsibilities, monitor progress, and provide simple reports for senior management to show success and obstacles.

## Step 5: Execute and lead.

The single most important element of governance and controls success is 100 percent buy-in from the senior team. High-level executives set the tone from the top, communicating the critical role of a governance and controls framework, recognizing and rewarding talent for identifying and addressing risks as they occur. It may take quarters, if not years, to implement the full framework, but once it's in place, you'll have the controls infrastructure to easily pass any vendor due diligence and snuff out or mitigate key risks.

## 5 Quick Risk-Control Tips

**Data security:** Lock this down before you build out your suite of technologies. Look at file and email encryption, password-protected portals, firewalls for network protection, secure remote access, virus protection, cloud based security, video monitoring of office and disaster recovery sites.

**Insurance:** Get this in place, considering Errors and Omissions, Directors and Officers, Property and Casualty and Key Man insurance. Work with a broker to determine what you need to protect your greatest assets and your balance sheet.

**Cash movements and accounting:** Require dual signatures and verbal approvals on cash movements, key fob to access accounts. Someone outside of finance should approve wire transfers. And a system such as Quick Books or Concur can allow you to move off spreadsheets and into a more robust system that provides oversight and monitoring of accounting and finances as well as time tracking for employees.

**Controls audit and financials audit:** Every year or other year, hire an outside firm to conduct an audit. A few professionals with fresh eyes can make all the difference in finding future risks and vulnerabilities.

**Social media policy:** To address one facet of reputational risk, be sure to lock down a strict social media policy. You don't want an employee's social life crossing into firm life lest the outside world view your firm very differently than you want it to. This applies to LinkedIn, Facebook, Snapchat or any other social site.

# CHAPTER 11

GETTING STRATEGIC PLANNING TO WORK FOR YOUR GROWING ENTERPRISE

I will never forget my first research assignment: compare and contrast three 19th century American authors.

I was in 11th grade, and Mr. Hollins assigned us to 1) do our research by reading at least three novels, 2) develop a thesis, 3) build an outline and 4) write a 15-page paper.

The process of writing a paper was easy compared to building the outline. Having an outline forced me to keep organized, make sure my points and quotes were supporting a point I was making, and make sure all the points supported my thesis.

In many ways, creating a 5-year strategic plan involves a very similar process to creating a good research paper outline:

1) Get all of your information together
2) Create a goal for where the company wants to go that is aligned with the corporate vision
3) Develop strategies to help you get there, and
4) Come up with specific tasks that can be accomplished to make it all happen.

For growing businesses, reaching an ambitious goal is difficult and painful without developing a focused strategic plan. The formal brainstorming process will align the senior team by getting agreement as to how resources will be deployed, where the company is headed and ownership for who will do which tasks. Once a strategic plan is mapped, functional and individual goals can cascade into the organization, and you can begin coordinating with the financial plan.

These four steps will help you create a planning process that will give your company the greatest chance to reach its potential.

## Step 1: Build the "front end".

Start by creating a "front end," which is basically the business to date. Consider the same sections you would for any business plan:

- History of the firm
- Product offerings
- Customers
- SWOT analysis
- Competitive analysis
- Key milestones
- Outlook for the industry
- Market size
- Market share
- Financials

Lastly, create future predictions for the company and industry. This will prove to be very useful when developing your actual plan. It can be challenging to write the history of the firm for the very first time. Meet this challenge by allowing a key team to divide and conquer various sections for a first draft.

Draft a separate front end for each segment of your business, as the markets and players are often very different.

Be prepared by setting aside time slots leading up to the planning session to develop and review the plan with the appropriate parties. Once complete, it is critical to review the front end with the entire leadership team in a single dedicated session to make sure that everyone is aligned. Then, and only then, can you move onto…

## Step 2: Build the "back end".

Now comes the fun part. Excel, Word, Google — it doesn't matter. It's all still an outline at the end of the day. Complete a separate back end for every front-end segment.

What is your **goal 5 years from now**?

- From that, write **3 objectives** that will help you reach that goal.
- Under each **objective**, write 6 strategies.
- Under each **strategy**, write 6 **tactics** — only the specific actions that you will take.

Definitions that will help guide you:

- A **goal** is a strategic thrust for the business, such as "become the No. 1 realty firm in the country by 2019."
- An **objective** supports that goal, and needs to happen in order to make the goal come true. Examples might be to open a certain number of locations, hire a certain number of brokers, or hit certain financial metrics.

- A **strategy** is the effort that needs to get underway for the objectives to be met. These might include pillaging outside brokerage firms of their top talent, or hiring hundreds of top MBA students.
- A **tactic** is a specific action that needs to happen to support that strategy. Examples might include attending a September career fair at a nearby business school, or setting up two meetings a week with potential candidates.

So, if there is one goal with three objectives, of six strategies each, and six tactics for each strategy, you will have 1 x 3 x 6 x 6= 108 specific tasks to track and complete. Keeping to a tight 1-3-6-6 framework will keep your energies focused and achievable. Putting in too much is like writing a rambling research paper that never really gets to the point.

Strategic Thrust: To become the dominant e-commerce firm focused on socks in the US

Objective 1: increase online presence

Strategy A: Build and roll out new website

| | Task | Responsible Party | Task Force | Status | 2018 | | | |
|---|---|---|---|---|---|---|---|---|
| | | | | | Q1 | Q2 | Q3 | Q4 |
| Tactic 1 | ———————— | ————— | ———— | Complete | | X | | |
| Tactic 2 | ————————————— | ———— | ———— | Not Complete | | | X | |
| Tactic 3 | ———————————— | ———— | ———— | Not Complete | | | | X |
| Tactic 4 | ———————— | ———— | ———— | Complete | X | | | |

Strategy B: Roll out social media effort to target 25-25 year demographic

| | Task | Responsible Party | Task Force | Status | 2018 | | | |
|---|---|---|---|---|---|---|---|---|
| | | | | | Q1 | Q2 | Q3 | Q4 |
| Tactic 1 | ———————— | ————— | ————— | Not Complete | | X | | |
| Tactic 2 | ————————————— | ———— | ————— | Complete | X | | | |
| Tactic 3 | ————————— | ———— | ————— | Not Complete | | X | | |
| Tactic 4 | ———————— | ———— | ————— | Not Complete | | | X | |

## Step 3: Assign ownership, and set due dates.

A single owner is ultimately responsible for accountability and delivery. A task force may step in, but this owner is in charge.

Assign a fiscal quarter by which you plan to accomplish the goal. This forces the individual to take responsibility for not only accomplishing the task, but also doing it on time! Some of the tasks might be targeted for this year, and others further out.

What's key is that you now have your outline.

## Step 4: Designate a facilitator and set a regular review process.

Designate a facilitator who will keep tangents to a minimum and conversation on track. Consider quarterly reviews, which can be part of monthly executive meetings or quarterly off-sites. You can easily declare what has been done, not done, or not done and not rescheduled. Otherwise, the team should sit around the table at a dedicated time to review the plan and see what has been accomplished, what needs to come off the plan, and what needs to be added. Then, at the end of each year, the front end planning can begin again. Repeat.

Before you jump into integrating strategic planning, you need 100 percent buy-in from all leadership. Don't half-ass it, or it will crumble fast. Do you have accountability for all the plans you put in place? Are goals and tactics aligned? In strategic planning meetings, phones, egos, and other work matters should be left behind. Set a tone for open dialogues, and be ready for the internal friction that may be required to create the company pearl.

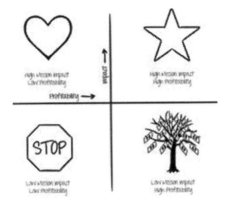

# CHAPTER 12

## 5 MAPPING TOOLS FOR STRATEGIC SUCCESS

The No. 1 killer of a successful business strategy? It's not an outside threat, it's an inside one, and it's called a lack of focus.

We all know the drill: We're at a retreat in Tulum, ostensibly to talk about the next 5 years, but we get sidetracked by the chitchat about travel and taco toppings. Or, we're sequestered in our Manhattan offices, aiming to ID our goals for the year ahead, and the conversation turns to various competitors' antics in the market.

There's a different approach, however, that can pull these strategic meetings together, keep you organized, and all your team to capture the key strategic components of the company while focusing on the most critical pieces of a truly successful business.

This new approach includes 5 mapping tools that can be customized to analyze any high-level strategic summary. They've worked for me. Here's how they can work for you.

## 1. SWOT Analysis

The Strengths, Weaknesses, Opportunities and Threats (SWOT) Analysis has become a favorite one for just about every business school geek to whip out. There's a reason why: it's legit. The strengths and weaknesses are more internally focused while opportunities and threats are more externally focused. I've found that having a leadership team filling this out before a retreat can be much more thought-provoking and capture more elements than starting with a blank sheet of paper in a group setting.

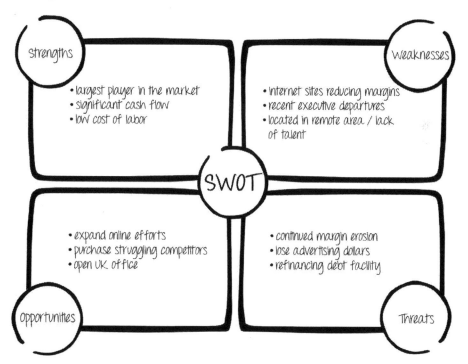

**strengths**
- largest player in the market
- significant cash flow
- low cost of labor

**weaknesses**
- internet sites reducing margins
- recent executive departures
- located in remote area / lack of talent

**SWOT**

**opportunities**
- expand online efforts
- purchase struggling competitors
- open UK office

**Threats**
- continued margin erosion
- lose advertising dollars
- refinancing debt facility

## 2. Risk Heat

This tool allows you to more closely examine Threats and Weaknesses. It's a simple, one-pager that puts the senior team on the same page by assessing if an event will happen, and what will the fallout will be if it does. The mapping framework allows the senior team to categorize any and all risks, from regulatory and legislative to legal and key employee retention, identifying which risks can be minimized and which ones must be absorbed. I've found it helpful to have participants list all the company's risks first, and then use the session discussion to move the risks around to the appropriate boxes.

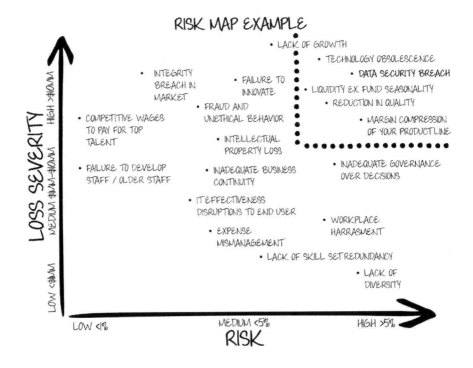

RISK MAP EXAMPLE

## 3. Internal Efforts

This tool shows the ease with which internal projects can be implemented, and their return on the project. It allows the senior team to see all the projects that are underway, and then to direct the appropriate discussions around prioritization and costs.

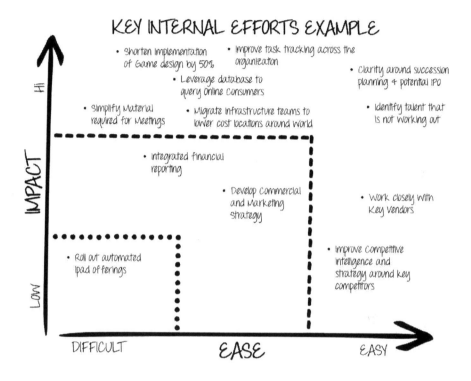

## 4. New Market Opportunities

Our fourth mapping tool allows you to dive into the current markets and potential opportunities, determining whether or not there is the technology or infrastructure to actually be successful. If you choose to venture into a more uncertain market, be very careful not to spend too long investing time and money. (Fail cheap and fail fast!) This mapping tool is typically where you can see all the ways a firm can grow top-line growth including organic, product expansion, geographic expansion, untapped revenue streams, acquisitions and joint ventures.

## NEW MARKET OPPORTUNITIES

- Launch a tech driven, 99.9% automated solution
- move into other Gaming Services
- move into international
- Enter 3-D virtual reality

OPTIONS (Fail early/ fail cheap)

- move into new geographies
- cross sell new products to existing client base
- offer menu of options and offerings
- Purchase other related businesses

CORE BUSINESS
- Charge subscription based fee
- Focus on newest emerging markets

Technology- can we do it? (Certain — uncertain)

Do we believe there is a market? (Certain — Uncertain)

## 5. Employee 9-Boxer

No retreat is over or year-end talent assessment is complete without a deep look into the employees. Using this map, the senior team can see if the internal talent is a consistent framework that allows cross-departmental view. Commonly known as the Employee 9-Boxer, the exercise puts each and every employee into one of nine boxes on a grid of performance and potential. It allows for thoughtful succession planning and compensation discussions, shows where you can make talent development decisions, and can also provide clarity around critical people issues.

# EMPLOYEE 9-BOXER GRID

|  | UNREALIZED POTENTIAL | EMERGING POTENTIAL | TOP TALENT |
|---|---|---|---|
| **ASSESSED POTENTIAL** | UNCERTAIN | WELL PLACED | HIGH ACHIEVER |
|  | STRONGEST CONCERN | SOLID CONTRIBUTER | PROVEN PERFORMER |

DEMONSTRATED PERFORMANCE

# CHAPTER 13

## KEEPING SHARP

I 've had that feeling plenty of times — the smallest things at work annoy me, my email box is full, people are coming to me with every problem and I can't seem to get everything in order. I'm stressed, angry, trapped and exhausted.

But if I'm able to recognize the symptoms early and do something about them, I can avoid a downward spiral that creeps into all areas of my life. Through many failures, I've found that doing a "check-in" across all areas of my life — professional, personal and spiritual — can be a good way to identify the opportunities to snap back into my regular energetic self.

Here are the tools that have worked for me.

# Professional

***Finding New Material:*** I try putting something fresh and interesting on my plate at work and delegate something that is draining. This constant reshuffling allows me to build a plate of work that is within my unique ability zone. Loving my work gives me energy instead of taking it away. This also helps me figure out what types of people to hire to take on and enjoy the work that I don't.

***Protecting my Calendar:*** I make sure that I am enforcing a "buffer day" when I can clean up all the outstanding to-do's. I try my best to protect this precious time on the calendar, or it drowns in the corporate wave of meetings and calls. I also try to plan all meetings for 50 minutes so I have space in between calls, meetings and work.

***Avoiding the GAP:*** I revisit my goals for the year ahead and break it down by quarter so I can see the small steps that I am making rather than how far away I am from the constantly increasing goals and expectations.

***Initiating energizing conversations:*** I look to use my lunches, commutes, breakfasts and coffee breaks to meet up with someone inside or outside of the office. These conversations can often be the highlight of my day and brings me the energy that I need to get through a challenging project or stressful period.

***Having an advisory group:*** I have several people that I have come to trust to share the most challenging situations at work. Whether it's a former boss or a member of the Young Presidents Organization, someone else can give me perspective on the issues that seem to be holding me back.

***Traps I can fall into:*** Saying "yes" to every meeting request; using my time on projects that will never go anywhere or will bring a low return on my time; or spending way too much time thinking about the same challenges repeatedly versus doing something about them.

# Personal

*Taking a vacation:* I see way too many people not use up their vacation days. I need a string of days off to refuel the energy tank so I can give my greatest amount of focus and effort.

*Rejuvenating during my time off:* When I do take a vacation, I make my favorite activities — hanging out with my wife and kids — a priority, and I create a flexible schedule. We might be at the beach, skiing, or golf. My wife and I both have big extended families so we try to even out time spent with each but, most importantly, have exclusive "protected" vacation time for only our immediate family. I try to come home a day early so I have time to unpack, check my emails and feel ready for the first day back.

*Putting something fun on my calendar:* Sometimes the best part of a vacation for me is simply knowing that there are a few fun days ahead of me. Spontaneous trips are great but I try to make sure I am excited about something on the calendar ahead.

*Interests outside of work:* I love hobbies — sports, projects, gardening. I like them because it gets my mind off of the gerbil wheel. A hobby can go a long way to relaxing my mind and restoring the energy tank.

*Giving back:* Some of my best friends and most enjoyable times are spent with a group of people that I help oversee fundraising events for the local hospital. I feel that my energy and talents can give back in a way that gives me positive energy and pleasure, which helps all other facets of my life.

*Meeting up with friends:* This is about planning social activities with the people that give me the most energy, make me laugh, or bring out a different side of me. Sometimes it's a simple dinner with my wife and another couple, or meeting up with an old friend I haven't reached out to for a while.

*Having a list of good podcasts, movies and documentaries:* I have a one-hour commute into work every day. Sometimes I work, but other times I like to relax and check out. Having this list, and a few movies already downloaded on my iPad, gives me the laughs and distraction that I need after a hard day at work.

*Enjoying date night with my wife:* This is one night every week or other week that my wife and I can just get out of the house, away from the bills, kids, and usual scenery for a good meal in town. It never has to be too fancy, just somewhere we can sit at the bar and catch up one-on-one.

*Eating well:* This is an obvious one, but something I can easily forget. I become aware of what I am putting into my body. The more health-giving it is, the better I feel.

*Exercise:* A good run or bike ride brings me the endorphins that I need. I occasionally use this time to think about challenges I'm facing and other times just to be mindful of the moment.

*Sleep:* I'm jealous of the people who can survive off of four hours of sleep. I can't. I need seven to eight hours, period. Anything less and I get moody, can't seem to focus as sharply and am tired. There are times that a few hours must do, but if I go for too long without my required sleep, I start dragging.

*Traps I can fall into:* Vacations that tire me out. Hanging out with people who bring me down, drinking too many glasses of wine or too much caffeine, eating a tub of Ben and Jerry's every night, not sleeping enough.

# Spiritual
For me, spirituality means personal space and mental balance.

*Mindfulness:* In the last two years, I have found mindfulness and meditation to be the most effective and significant positive impacts on my own mental balance. They help me avoid dwelling on the future or the past, and give me the balance I need to make important decisions on behalf of the organization.

*Reading:* I enjoy having a good book at my bedside. I can't guarantee I will remember every character, but I can follow along and get caught in a different mindset before falling asleep. Book dreams are better than work dreams.

*Sunday Un-plug:* Spending my Sunday offline with my family can often mean the difference between a great week and a burnout. Taking my kids and my dog for a walk in the park, going to church, or simply relaxing for the week ahead is rejuvenating for me and my entire family. The day gives me the peace and time to reflect on how grateful and lucky I am to even be in this world. The omnipresent iPhone is hidden away for at least five hours.

*Traps I can fall into:* I forget about all the above and I start dwelling on my problems instead of finding that important space so I can put things into perspective and potentially approach my work challenges from different angles.

## Execution

While many of these pieces sound simple, I often find them challenging to practice consistently. So I pick my spots and get the professionals I need. Mindfulness can be close to impossible for me alone, so my wife and I have a mindfulness and yoga coach who comes to our home every Sunday and spends time with our kids and us. In the winter I have a fitness coach who meets with me for one hour a week. I look at these costs as investments in me. The sharper I can be at work, the better I will perform.

I track the above and rank them 1 to 10 and do a check-in once a week to see what progress I have made. It's a great way to make sure I'm staying on track. Adding the positive elements into my life and taking out the negatives is a reshuffling that can not only help me get out of a work rut but also significantly reduce underlying stress and bring me greater fulfillment in my overall life.

# BONUS CHAPTER

## 11 Tips for Launching An Executive Career

A few years ago, I sat down with a 24-year-old woman who worked on our quantitative analysis team. She was clearly miserable doing financial modeling for insurance policies, so I asked her what she really wanted to do. "Become an equity analyst," she said. We agreed that her time would be better spent pursuing her passion than performing work that did not energize her—and today, much to my delight, she's a successful equity analyst.

That's just one example of how I get great satisfaction working with recent college graduates who are at critical junctures in their lives. If you are in your 20s, chances are you'll make decisions now that will affect what you'll do and where you'll live for your entire career. Here's how to navigate them.

## 1. Be honest with yourself.

Right before the recession of 2008-09, I was working at a credit hedge fund, raising capital and analyzing new credits. It seemed like an ideal job at the time — I worked close to home, got paid well and enjoyed learning. But when the economy sank, I forced myself to take a deeper look into what I enjoyed. I realized it had nothing to do with analyzing credits; it had more to do with building a business and working with people to make a vision come alive. I accepted both a pay cut and a new one-hour commute to pursue a profession that continues to be rewarding and energizing every day.

## 2. Decide whether you need another degree or certification.

You typically have more flexibility in your 20s than in your 30s. This is the time to figure out whether you need another degree or certification to master a subject matter. When I was 27, I left the workforce to go to business school, because I wanted to learn more about all facets of business, and I wanted to be around other like-minded professionals. Someone else may choose to get an RN, PhD, EMT, or CFA. But whatever the letters are, obtaining those degrees spells more complications and greater expenses the further you are in your life and career.

## 3. Get involved with your community.

I've met many of my best friends through community efforts. What are you passionate about? Volunteer work allows you to meet new people and engage with your surroundings in new and stimulating ways. You'll pick up new skills, too; for me, it was leadership, project management and fundraising — all critical to my career.

## 4. Make a development plan.

Having a development plan is key for any ambitious professional. Mine details my mission, three-year plan, and specific strategies for my goals.

People, training, conferences, networking events, and community service projects can give you the skills you need to advance to the next level. This approach helps me see how I'm growing professionally and personally.

## 5. Network.

No matter what role you have, building a network is critical. But networking doesn't feel natural for most of us, so put yourself out there. Once you do, you'll realize how colorful and interesting other people are. Use LinkedIn, send an email, pick up the phone, send a letter — but be proactive about it. You never know where the next opportunity will be, but chances are it will be from someone you know. Ask each person you meet for three new contacts so that your circle continues to widen. Build networking into your daily or weekly list of to-dos.

## 6. Read, read, read (and watch some TV).

Curiosity and a love of learning separates workers from leaders. What topics interest you, and how can you master them? Cut out unhealthy distractions. Instead, listen to audiobooks during your commute, read blogs at lunchtime, subscribe to newspapers and periodicals, and watch documentaries and TED talks related to your career. Follow up on subjects and people. A click of the button can lead you to learn from the experts in your field. Never before have we had so much information available to us. Tap into it and see where it takes you!

## 7. Find a mentor.

Having someone you can turn to at specific stages of your work life can be your most powerful asset. I followed my father into a similar profession, and he has been a huge influence on my own life and career. He's my go-to person to bounce around ideas, seek advice and vent. Find a natural connection and ask if you can reach out on a regular basis. You'll be surprised at how willing people are to help.

## 8. Build your own personal board.

Once you've found a mentor, seek others who can serve as regular sounding boards or advisors for other facets of your life. Life is a lot easier when you have others to guide you, and it's a lot more fun knowing that you're not alone. I found my own board through work, community service projects, being part of a presidents' association, and a school alumni network. Some are in my field and others are not. But they're all helpful as I grow professionally and personally.

## 9. Build your own personal brand.

If you don't tell people who you are and what you're good at, no one can help you. Figure out how to articulate what you do. To start, revisit your résumé and make it your personal flyer. Develop your personal elevator pitch so that you can tell people quickly what you do and what you're looking to do. Having examples of what you achieved means others can see your value.

## 10. Exceed expectations with excellence.

First, exceed your own expectations — then you will exceed others'. Very early in my transition to management at CIT Group, I got the overwhelming feeling that I would get lost in the company's thousands of employees and never get adequate recognition. It did not take long for me to realize this was a dead-end state of mind. So, instead, I focused that energy on delivering the absolute best product I could, no matter what the task. A month or so after my attitude readjustment, I delivered a presentation highlighting the company's overvalued lending book and its incentive system that was misaligned to the stated risk tolerance of the firm. The firm quickly shared the presentation around, and in just a few days, I found myself presenting to the entire senior leadership team. Four weeks later, I was working at the firm's headquarters as the COO of Risk. It was my first real breakthrough into senior management. So instead of thinking about how you can get ahead, aim to consistently deliver an A+ product.

## 11. Raise your hand.

There are no better employees than those who raise their hands to take on more work. It is filling in the cracks that enables you to take on leadership roles and get some well-deserved recognition. These one-off projects can be that extra little push that moves you from a 9.5 player to a perfect 10. Get your hands dirty and grab the projects that are interesting, new, and put you in contact with other natural leaders in your organization.

# ALEX TUFF

A lex has been President of Winged Keel Group since joining in 2013. He has more than 18 years of executive experience in the financial services industry. In addition to overseeing and managing all business functions and employees, Alex serves as a member of Winged Keel Group's Executive Management Committee. Prior to Winged Keel, Alex spent five years as the COO of the 650-person Risk Management Group at CIT.

Alex is a member of the Fairchester Chapter of the Young Presidents Organization (YPO). As a member of Stamford Hospital's Board of Directors, he has served on both the Finance and Strategy Committees, and currently serves on the Foundation Board of Stamford Hospital, focusing energy on fundraising for a new regional hospital. Additionally, he is the founder and chair of an endowed scholarship for the benefit of high school students that have lost one or both parents. Alex promotes the ongoing dialogue of leadership topics as a contributor to the alumni magazine of Columbia Business School. Alex has also been a featured lecturer at Brown University on leadership and management topics.

Alex earned an MBA in Finance with Distinction from Columbia Business School and a BA in Economics from Colby College. Alex and his wife, Liz, reside in New Canaan, Connecticut, with their three children. He is an avid skier and golfer, plays competitive paddle tennis, and coaches youth soccer.

Made in the USA
Columbia, SC
13 September 2018